Oxford Gargoyles

A Little Souvenir

CHRIS ANDREWS PUBLICATIONS

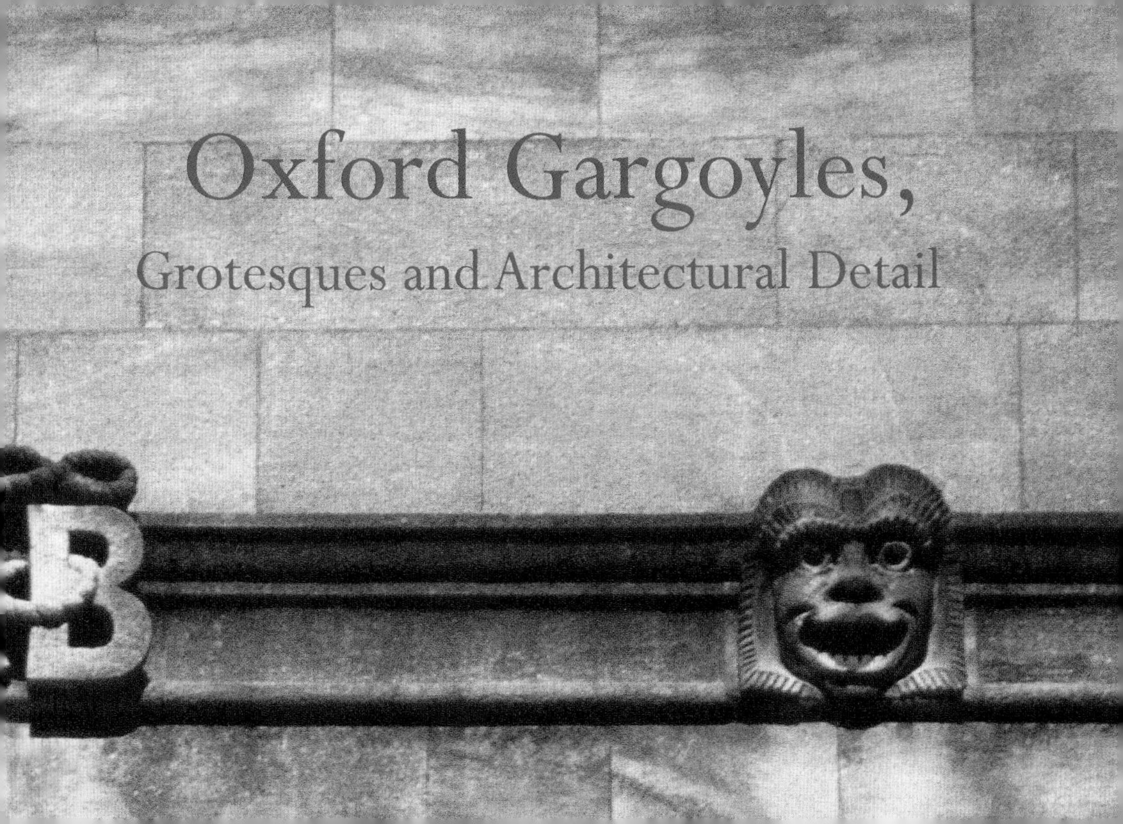

Oxford Gargoyles,

Grotesques and Architectural Detail

Introduction

Oxford is noted as one of England's cultural, educational and architectural masterpieces – its history as a settlement reaches back before the year 1000 AD. Its history academically may be said to begin in the 1100's when King Henry's quarrel with the french prevented scholars from attending the university in Paris.

Oxford is familiar for the wealth of architectural variety and quality which has accompanied its development, its vast vistas, majestic spires, remarkable colleges and university buildings. Yet it has wealth in detail as well - strange creatures in stone roam along and around the buildings. The stone carvings of Oxford show variety and quality, a range of subjects and functions, they can be as fascinating as the more famous 'spires and groves'.

Gargoyles are carvings that have a function - they take the rain from the guttering behind them, 'gargling' it and spewing it out through the mouth. A Grotesque is a figure

A true gargoyle 5

with a grotesque character – possibly of humour or horror, but with a decorative function, and perhaps to scare away evil spirits. Both may be human or animal, allegorical or real, they may represent noted individuals or religious figures - the latter reflecting the root of their construction in the Middle Ages when it became popular to decorate churches and cathedrals. Other examples of the stonemasons art can be seen in numerous small details: crests, niches, statuary, decoration and embellishment.

6 Some carvings seem to send a message

Almost all involve the viewer in looking up, they are to be seen against the skyline and on top of the spires, along college buildings, on church and chapel towers. Some are inside, most outside. The Bodleian Library has an especially great variety and quality, but most if not all university and college buildings have a range.

These carvings are usually made from the same stone as the building they adorn, some are hidden,

The baroque portico on the High Street front of St Mary's Church

8 Carved angel in Oriel College

but most are on prominent display and they excite comment: In 1125 St. Bernard of Clairvaux complained to a fellow abbot, "Of what use to the brothers reading piously in the cloisters are these ridiculous monstrosities, these prodigies of deformed beauty, these beautiful deformities? Almighty God! If we are not ashamed of these unclean things, we should at least regret what we have spent on them." While the monks debated the carvers carved. In recent times Oxford has benefited from master masons and sculptors such as William Orchard,

Michael Black, Michael Grose, Percy Quick, Thomas Tyrell, E.S. Frith, Kenneth Gardner and more, we are fortunate to see their legacy, the images challenge and delight as much today as when they were installed.

10 Self-portrait of a stone mason, New College Chapel

12 “Quiet!” The Bodleian Library

A collection of carvings on Magdalen College Tower

14 Is this carving making comment?

Corner stone on Wadham College

16 ‘See no evil’ and perhaps ‘seeing evil’, New College

Man and beast seem equally fascinated

18 A witness observes Eve and the Forbidden Apple, New College

Long face, New College

20 The Monkeys of New College

A 'Grotesque' Bat

22 Charity, one of the Seven Virtues series, New College

Innocent Love of the Seven Virtues, New College

24 Window decoration on the Bodleian Library

Carvings on the Bodleian Library looking towards the Clarendon Building

26 Intricate creations on St John's College

An eyeful in Magdalen College Cloisters

28 St John's College, perhaps a portrait?

A Grotesque on the Bodleian Library, probably not a portrait

30 A grotesque emerging from the stone and a harvester, Magdalen College

The romance of Magdalen College

32 The intricate ceiling of the Divinity Schools

Cardinal Wolsey flanked by angels on The Wolsey Tower, Christ Church

34 Clockwise from top left: details on Magdalen, Balliol, Magdalen and St John's Colleges

A trio of carvings on Magdalen College

36 Carvings on St John's College flank an alarmed head

38 Possibly a miller with a heavy sack?

Barely hanging on at the Bodleian Library

40 Two figures in Balliol College representing vice!, this one drunkeness,

42 Decorations on the original gateway to Trinity College

A lion and a lady on Hertford and Wadham Colleges

44 The Coat of Arms of King Charles II above the Sheldonian Theatre north door

Carved stone head outside the Sheldonian Theatre

46 Protecting a nest, or preying on it?

A bearded figure peers down from Merton College

The carved tympanum over Merton College gateway

50 A winged grotesque

A watchful dog on the Bodleian Library

52 Looking up at the Ashmolean Museum

Looking up at the western front of All Souls College

54 Was the carving designed to enhance this view of the Radcliffe Camera?

Hertford College crest and carvings on the Bridge of Sighs

56 Jesus College crest

The Royal Arms of Queen Victoria on the High Street front of Brasenose College

58 Embellishments on the Modern History Faculty

Fan vaulting and decoration in University College

60 Spectacular lead work in St John's College

A D
19 52

EST REPOSITA JUSTITÆ CORONA
PRÆSIDE THOMA TURNER

LOGIC LANE

62 Carving on the Modern History Faculty

King James I with the University and Fame, Tower of the Old Schools Quad

First published 2006 reprinted 2009, 2011, 2013

by

Chris Andrews Publications, 15 Curtis Yard, North Hinksey Lane, Oxford, OX2 0LX

Telephone: +44(0)1865 723404 email: enquiries@cap-ox.com. **www.cap-ox.com**

ISBN 978 1 905385 14 0

Acknowledgement

Many thanks for permission to quote from *Oxford's Gargoyles and Grotesques* by John Blackwood and David Collett (1986)

Front Cover: See No Evil, New College Title page: Churchillian Dragon, Magdalen College P2/3: Carvings on the Bodleian Library